CUT

THE **MERCY FOR** SERIES

CUT

Mercy for Self-Harm

NANCY ALCORN

WINEPRESS WP PUBLISHING

WinePress Publishing (PO Box 428, Enumclaw, WA 98022) functions only as book publisher. As such, the ultimate design, content, editorial accuracy, and views expressed or implied in this work are those of the author.

ISBN 13: 978-1-57921-897-3
ISBN 10: 1-57921-897-0
Library of Congress Catalog Card Number: 2007921239

ENDORSEMENTS

I know all too well how the world places an overemphasis on what we see on the outside, and girls often resort to self-destructive patterns. I personally support the work of Mercy Ministries because I have seen firsthand the changed lives.

—**Niki Taylor**
International Supermodel

As a father of two girls in their late teens, I certainly know what girls face today. I have watched Nancy Alcorn and Mercy Ministries bring hope and healing to struggling young women for many years—young women who were completely without hope. The *Mercy for . . .* series reveals the Mercy Ministries difference and offers great inspiration, hope, and a way to true healing for all who want to be free.

—**Dave Ramsey**
Financial Expert and Author of *The Total Money Makeover*

Nancy Alcorn offers young women hope—to have self-esteem and grow in wholeness—and more. Mercy Ministries is not afraid to deal with the tough, ugly stuff. If you are a young woman struggling with these issues, or if you have a daughter or work with girls, you want to hear what Nancy has to say. It is sure to change your life!

—**CeCe Winans**
Grammy Award-Winning Recording Artist

I have personally known young women who have found healing through the principles in these books. This series is very timely in an age where little hope is given for young women struggling with these issues. Nancy Alcorn is not afraid to tell the truth and offer real hope through forgiveness and restoration. If you are desperate for hope or affected by a hopeless life, read through this series and find real answers.

—**Sue Semrau**
Head Women's Basketball Coach, Florida State University

DEDICATION

To those who are **desperate** for help
but feel there is no hope.
This book has been placed in your **hands** for a reason—
it is no accident that you are reading this even now.
My **prayer** is that you will read on,
because this book was written for you.
If you receive its message,
you will **never** be the same!
—*Nancy Alcorn*

TABLE OF CONTENTS

ACKNOWLEDGEMENTS

I would like to thank the Mercy Ministries staff who have spent countless hours working on this manuscript with a heart to help people—Sherry Douglas, Cassidy Carlgren, Cissy Etheridge, Janelle Pharis, Ashley Cupples, Amanda Goldsberry, and Sarah Dixon.

Thanks to the Mercy residents who read the manuscripts and provided honest feedback, helping to ensure the most helpful and relevant material.

A heartfelt thanks to our friends and supporters throughout the world who give so generously to bring forth changed lives.

Last but not least, I have such gratitude for our faithful staff in the various homes around the world. They give so much every day, and their love and compassion is evident. Thanks for serving alongside me in this global vision. You guys amaze me!

All royalties and profits from this book will go back into the work of Mercy Ministries around the world.

SPECIAL THANKS . . .

To Holly, whose life has been completely and totally transformed. We want to honor you for allowing us to use your picture on the cover of this book because of your desire to see other young women experience the freedom that you have experienced. The fact that you now know that you are not forgotten inspires me to continue reaching others.

I also wish to thank Holly's mother, who wrote the following endorsement for this book . . .

"I think that this book is very relevant and includes all the information I was looking for a few years ago. With Holly, first the cutting started, then the vicious cycle of sexual abuse which led to sin and immorality and shame, which kept the cutting going. So I was never quite sure which problem came first.

Holly is doing awesome back home. She is beautiful and transformed by Jesus. We love her so much. She really misses everyone at Mercy. Her prayer here at home is to make new friends and get connected with a college small group at church. We would love your prayers for Holly."

INTRODUCTION

I couldn't stop myself. I had to cut. Not cutting meant everything was okay, and everything was anything but okay. So dead inside, I picked up a blade and glided it across my thigh.

—Lindsay

*L*indsay couldn't take the silent suffering any longer. She had no way to express the pain she felt or the sense of being a prisoner to it, except through self-harm. If she could not feel anything on the inside, she had to prove to herself she could at least feel something on the outside.

Just like Lindsay, millions of people of all ages wrestle with the seemingly inescapable problem of self-harm on a daily basis. Out-of-control emotions or the inability to feel at all may result in self-harm behaviors, such as cuts, burns, bruises, or worse.

Does this scenario describe someone you love who is struggling with self-harm on a regular basis, or does it describe you? Are you desperate for answers?

There are many girls, just like you or someone you know, wanting a way out. Many have found it, and you will read some of their stories. Since 1983, Mercy Ministries has served more than two thousand young women from across the country and from varied cultural and economic backgrounds.

Young women who come to Mercy Ministries are often facing a combination of difficult circumstances, and many of them have sought prior treatment without successful long-term results, yet they graduate from the Mercy Ministries program truly transformed. They are found attending universities, working in ministries and in corporations, on the mission field, and at home raising families. Our residents are young women who want to change and move beyond their difficult circumstances, yet have never been able to before. But at Mercy Ministries, they find hope.

You can find hope too. This book was written to give you more understanding of your struggle and help you learn practical ways to acknowledge, identify, and eliminate self-harm from your life. There is hope, there is freedom, and there is mercy for self-harm.

Chapter One

WHAT IS SELF-HARM?

When you look at the word *self-harm*, you might picture a scene from a horror movie, but the reality is that self-harm—a deliberate, repetitive, impulsive harming of the body—is mainly done in secret and can sometimes be hard to detect.

For example, Nikki, a college student, receives a below-average score on an important exam. This hits her hard; the perfection she demands of herself screams accusations in her mind. When she arrives home, she is so distraught with herself that she takes a razor blade and begins to make small cuts on her leg and thigh where the marks cannot be seen. By punishing herself, she feels a release.

Jamie's mother yells at her for not doing the dishes correctly, and Jamie feels, once again, that she never does anything right. She runs to her room, takes out a pencil, and begins to rub burns on her arm and stomach as punishment. When she comes out of her room, the burns are hidden by her shirt.

Becky has been abused, and she's tried everything she knows to get rid of the pain that torments her constantly. She has starved herself and tried bulimia, over-exercising, and more. The only thing left, she thinks, that might relieve the pain inside the darkest chambers of her life is to try to bring that pain outside. She cuts and waits, anticipating that release will come.

You may be thinking, *I know someone who does that* or *I do that, but it's really not a big deal.* However, if you are inflicting any self-harming behavior on yourself, it *is* a big deal.

Signs and Symptoms

Self-harm is the outward expression of pain and hurt deep within. Some of the signs and symptoms of self-harming behavior look like this:

- Inflicting cuts with any type of sharp object, usually on an area of the body not normally exposed
- Constant scratching as a response to pressure or unexpected circumstances
- Picking at scabs and preventing the healing process from taking place
- Burning the skin on a regular basis with erasers, fire, or small heat-conducting appliances or metals
- Punching the body, including beating the head against walls or other inanimate objects
- Biting the inside of the mouth or the skin of the arms, hands, or legs
- Pulling hair out—including eyelashes and eyebrows
- Breaking bones or severely bruising the body

Girls minimize self-harm by saying things such as "I only pick at my skin sometimes when I am emotional" or "Well, at least I don't really hurt myself, like break my leg or something. It's just a cut here and there. It's just a nervous habit." But the truth is: if you are cutting, burning, bruising, biting, chewing, scratching, or purposefully harming yourself in any way, you are struggling with self-harm.

Behind the Behavior

We all have different ways of handling stressful and discouraging events in our lives, but self-harm should never be an option. So how does self-harm start, and why do you do it?

Self-harm begins when you feel controlled by the pain in your life. A girl who self-injures sees a need to alleviate the pain of her circumstances and believes that self-harm is the only way to accomplish that. With this distorted view of reality, everything in her life becomes skewed. Often loved ones, close friends, and even God are replaced by the destructive behavior.

How does something so harmful and damaging seem to bring relief? The reasons lie underneath the behavior. The roots of self-harm must be dealt with and removed in order to experience true freedom.

Destructive Emotions

Girls who self-harm often do it to communicate feelings and emotions they don't know how to verbalize. Anxiety, fear, loneliness, nervousness, and anger are some of the destructive emotions girls try to deal with by choosing to self-injure.

When you are in a situation that is stressful, what emotions rise up within you? What do you do with these emotions? You may try to find a way to relieve the intensity of what you are feeling, or you may try to avoid feeling altogether. Self-harm is a response to circumstances that cause overwhelming emotions you feel you cannot handle without creating external release.

Escape

If you use any type of self-harm as a means of escape from reality, you have adopted a self-destructive coping mechanism for dealing with life.

Escaping reality is one of the main causes of self-harm. You might feel like you are bringing the emotional pain from the inside to the outside. You are hurting, so you cut to relieve the pain, but the hurt is still there when the outward pain is gone. Self-harm only provides a temporary escape.

Past or Present Abuse

Abuse is closely tied to self-harm. When you experience traumatic events such as sexual, verbal, and physical abuse, it can be very difficult for you to make sense of your emotions and know how to handle them. This is especially true if you are in an environment where you feel you must remain silent. The condemnation and feelings of guilt and shame cause many girls to begin to cut because they hate themselves for what they have endured. Whether you think you deserve punishment because of what has happened or you simply aren't able to deal with the emotional trauma you are experiencing, self-harm provides a false sense of release.

> *You know, I just wanted to see blood. I have no idea why, but I needed to see blood. I was drawn to it because if I could make myself bleed, it made me think I had hurt enough. I had been abused and no one believed me. I could never tell anyone, so I suffered in silence for many years, punishing myself for what I thought was weakness and inadequacy.*
>
> —Sarah

Sarah was not allowed to talk about the abuse she was experiencing, and she didn't because she was afraid. This caused her to punish herself for those exact reasons: fear, inadequacy, and weakness. In reality, she was neither weak nor inadequate, but she thought she was. Self-harm seemed to be all she had.

Family Dysfunction

Families should be a source of support and encouragement, yet this is not the case in everyone's life. Some girls grow up in the midst of divorce, drug and alcohol addictions, or severe abuse. Being exposed to these types of behaviors can be very damaging to anyone at any age.

Though less severe, growing up in a family that is argumentative, very sarcastic, or very distant emotionally can also cause serious problems. If you are never encouraged and you are always put down by sarcastic comments, if the family atmosphere is volatile and you never know what to expect, or if family members never seem to care or connect with one another, then self-harm may have become a way of dealing with the situations you face and the things you feel.

Depression

The signs of depression are usually consistent over a period of time and shouldn't be confused with the emotions you feel after a bad day. These signs can include feeling hopeless or pessimistic or sad, losing interest in hobbies and activities that you used to enjoy, difficulty concentrating, insomnia, changes in appetite, restlessness, and irritability. Depression can seem to consume your life and your mind.

Extreme hopelessness and sadness are catalysts for self-harm. Why? Depression can make you feel like you have no way out and things will never change. You may believe that you are unable to learn how to cope with life. Depression and self-harm can be a dangerous life-threatening combination.

Shame

Shame makes you feel that you deserve punishment. It may compel you to believe that you are worthless and deserve the very worst. Shame is relentless, grabbing you and holding on for dear life.

What are the things in your life that make you feel sick to your stomach when you think about them? Those feelings could be fostering self-harm. Are there things in your past that you have never shared with anyone due to fear and shame? First Peter 5:8 says, "Be well balanced (temperate, sober of mind), be vigilant and cautious at all times; for that enemy of yours, the devil, roams around like a lion roaring [in fierce hunger], seeking someone to seize upon and devour" (AMP). Satan, your enemy, wants you to remain speechless, voiceless, and trapped. This is a tactic he uses to keep things hidden in your life to prevent you from dealing with the root causes. He knows that if you expose these things that have caused shame in your life, you will break his power over you.

Doesn't My Body Belong to Me?

You may be thinking, *Okay, yeah, I self-harm, but I've got good reasons, and doesn't my body belong to me? Can't I do whatever I want with it?*

No!

Imagine that someone built you the house of your dreams. Everything about it was beautiful, ornate, and designed specifically for you. The thought of someone entering your home with a chainsaw and destroying all that had been so carefully crafted is horrifying! Watching someone shred curtains, punch holes in the walls, and obliterate your home would be devastating to you, and that's how it is for God to see you purposefully destroy your own body.

God uniquely designed you as His beautiful masterpiece. Psalm 139:13–16 says:

> You shaped me first inside, then out;
>   you formed me in my mother's womb.
> I thank you, High God—you're breathtaking!
>   Body and soul, I am marvelously made!
>   I worship in adoration—what a creation!
> You know me inside and out,
>   you know every bone in my body;
> You know exactly how I was made, bit by bit,
>   how I was sculpted from nothing into something.
> Like an open book, you watched me grow from conception
>   to birth; all the stages of my life were spread out before
>   you,
> The days of my life all prepared
>   before I'd even lived one day (MSG).

God's love is so much more than we can comprehend. He desires your freedom so much that He sent His Son to die for it. "You do not belong to yourself, for God bought you with a high price. So you must honor God with your body" (1 Corinthians 6:19–20, NLT). Romans 12:1 says, "Take your everyday, ordinary life—your sleeping, eating, going-to-work, and walking-around life—and place it before God as an offering. Embracing what God does for you is the best thing you can do for him" (MSG).

Self-Harm Is a Cycle

Every time I cut, I thought the release I felt would make my pain go away. But afterwards I was just overwhelmed with shame and guilt. I felt trapped and continued to give in to the urge to cut, seeing no way out. It was a hellish cycle for six years.

—Aubrey

You may feel that you deserve punishment. You may hate yourself and want to die, but you are scared to follow through. You may be trying to make yourself feel something, anything, or maybe you really have no idea why you injure yourself . . . you just do. Whatever your situation, one thing is sure to be true: every time there is an overwhelming urge to hurt yourself, you give in to that urge.

It may seem like it is a never-ending cycle with no way out; however, this is not the case. You've tried to find your own way of escape and fallen into destructive behaviors, but the Word of God says that the Lord always provides a way of escape when we are tempted (1 Corinthians 10:13). God tells us to turn to Him when we are hurting because He wants to comfort us, restore our joy, and break the destructive cycle of self-harm that the devil wants us to believe is the only way to handle life's issues.

If you have family members who have not or will not work out problems, if there is any abuse, if you are dealing with depression or shame, or if you have no idea why you engage in self-harm, please seek help immediately. Start by talking with a strong, mature Christian (pastor, teacher, counselor, or friend), someone can you trust and confide in. God can use mature believers and spiritual leaders to demonstrate the unconditional acceptance and love available to you through Jesus.

The Bible talks about calling out to God when you are down to your last gasp, when you are so weak or feel so far away (Psalm 61:2). Ask God to give you the strength that comes from Christ (Philippians 4:13). Psalm 107:20 says, "By the power of his own word, he healed you and saved you from destruction" (CEV).

Chapter Two

BREAKING FREE

Now that I have dealt with all the abuse I endured, I am completely free from self-harm and I have no desire to go back! I know I am important and valuable to God, and that is priceless to me!

—Rochelle

*Y*ou might be thinking, *Okay, I see some of the possible roots of self-harm in my life, but how do I deal with these things?* God sees your pain and will meet you where you are. He is the only one who can touch your heart so deeply that your life can change.

The Bible tells us to go after what we need and never to give up in our pursuit for positive change. Luke 11:9 says, "Here's what I'm saying: ask and you'll get; seek and you'll find; knock and the door will open" (MSG). Bring all your questions to God, and He will lead you to the answers. Jeremiah 33:3 says, "Call to me and I will answer you. I'll tell you marvelous and wondrous things that you could never figure out on your own" (MSG).

God wants to help you. He created you and loves you unconditionally. He sees the pain inside that you are trying to release or express through abusing yourself. God has already paid the price for your sin. He sent His only Son, Jesus, to the cross as the ultimate sacrifice so that you would not have to bear the punishment we all deserve for our sins. When Jesus died, His blood cleansed and wiped away every sin you have committed or ever will commit. Jesus did not come to condemn you but to help you find freedom.

Your blood has no power, which is why self-harm is not the answer to your problems. In fact, harming yourself and believing that it is your responsibility to punish yourself is actually denying and rejecting the freedom Jesus offers you. It's like saying that the agony and torture Jesus went through on the cross was not enough.

Let's look at what can happen when you accept, rather than reject, the power of Jesus' shed blood.

Choose Love

The road to freedom begins with accepting Jesus as your Lord and Savior. This is the most important decision and choice you will ever make.

Have you asked Jesus to come into your life? If so, you need to follow Him now and develop a relationship with Him that is more than just a surface acquaintance. If not, all you have to do is ask Jesus to be your Savior and Lord over all of your life and to forgive you for the all the mistakes you have made. Jesus died on the cross to forgive all the sins in your past, present, and future. All you have to do is ask!

You may be thinking, *My sin is just too awful—Jesus may have died for the world, but not for me.* God would have sent Jesus to die if you were the only person on earth who needed to be saved; He loves you that much! You are His child, and what good parent wants to see His children hurting? Jesus came to set you free from guilt, shame, condemnation, self-hate, and self-harm. He wants to give you a new life full of joy and peace. Not only will He show you the root causes of your pain, He will help you deal with your emotions in new and healthy ways. Jesus will restore and transform your broken heart!

> *I have struggled with self-harm almost daily for the past three years. The self-hatred inside drove me to try to destroy myself. It wasn't until I decided to believe the truth about God's love for me and the fact that He created and designed me exactly the way I am for a reason, that my heart, mind, and desires started to change.*
>
> —Krystal

First, you have to trust Him and put your life in His hands. Ask Him into your heart and life today! Here is a sample prayer you can use:

Prayer for Salvation

Jesus, I am so lost. I don't know how I got so far from you, but I have. I need you, and I ask you to come into my heart. Save me! Change my heart. I believe you are the Son of God; I believe you died on a cross for my sin and shame. This day, I choose life. I choose you. I know that you will walk with me on this journey, so I can rest in knowing that you will help me through it all. In Jesus' name, Amen.

God will never hurt you or betray you. His love for you will never change because it is not based on your behavior but on His character, which is love and mercy.

Please know that you have a choice about whether to give in to self-harm or to surrender to God. The Bible says in Deuteronomy 30:19, "Today I have given you the choice between life and death, between blessings and curses" (NLT). This verse goes on to say that we are to choose life. With God there is a plan for your life that will bring joy and peace, but you must choose to follow His plan in order for it to work. The Bible says that God's desire right now is to set you free: "'For I know the plans I have for you,' says the Lord, 'they are plans for good and not for disaster, to give you a future and a hope'" (Jeremiah 29:11, NLT).

Verbalize Your Pain

Every person's process to freedom is different, but another important step toward healing is to verbalize the pain.

> *I was so scared to talk about those things in my past that I literally thought I was going to throw up at the thought of speaking it out loud. I wanted to forget it all together and leave it buried, definitely not remember it and speak it out loud. But the second I released it, I was totally free, and the power those memories had over me has been broken.*
>
> —Aubrey

Aubrey finally got to the place where the pain she was experiencing was greater than her shame. She confessed these things the enemy was using to torment her and received her freedom.

Those awful memories you have may lie dormant for a while, but they will always resurface, often at the worst possible time, and debilitate you. Whatever you are experiencing that has lured you into self-harm, you can break its hold over your life by immediately going to a counselor, teacher, pastor, or mature friend you can confide in and telling this person what is going on. Talking about it may be as hard for you as it was for Aubrey, but with God's help you can overcome.

Don't hesitate. Quickly expose your pain and receive the freedom the Lord is so excited to give you. He is a very safe place to take your pain, guilt, and shame. Allow yourself to trust Him with your wounds, because Psalm 62:6–8 says, "He's solid rock under my feet, breathing room for my soul, an impregnable castle: I'm set for life. My help and glory is in God—granite-strength and safe-harbor God—So trust him absolutely, people; lay your lives on the line for him. God is a safe place to be" (MSG).

Learning to communicate can be difficult, but to deal with your emotions in a healthy way you have to learn to talk about them. Talking can be hard at first, and it is okay to work your way there slowly. It might be easier for you to write down how you feel. Some girls communicate very well through writing poetry or journaling. Another way to express how you feel is by drawing or painting. When there seem to be no words to describe how you feel, a picture may help represent your emotions.

Invite Jesus to heal the broken places in your heart. Whether it stems from abuse, death of a loved one, or even a harsh word that has wounded your soul, Jesus sees your pain and wants to heal it. When a specific situation comes to mind that caused you pain, pray and talk to God about it. Share with Him how you feel and your frustrations about the situation. God already knows everything, but He loves when you spend time with Him and talk to Him about what is going on. He wants to heal the pain of your past. Allow yourself to be vulnerable and open as Jesus walks you through this process. He will bring peace to your heart as He restores every place of brokenness in your life. Here is a sample prayer you can use:

Prayer for Help and Healing

Lord, you are the only one who knows what is in the depths of my heart. You know the deepest secrets in my soul and the hurts and wounds of my life. I ask you to look into my heart now and bring to the surface what you want to heal. I ask you to reveal the root causes for self-harm in my life and give me the wisdom and grace to deal with them and give them to you. I ask you to come into my life and heal my heart and the wounds of my soul. Be my strength and bring the peace that only you can give. Cover me with your love and mercy. In Jesus' name, Amen!

Give Up Control

In order for me to get over my obsession with cutting myself, I had to first accept that I was loved by God. That acceptance process was really hard for me because I never thought anyone cared. Then, as I read the Word and cried out to God when I was tempted to hurt myself, God came and delivered me because I chose to surrender myself to Him.

—Jessie

Self-harm makes you feel that you are in control. However, just the opposite is true. When you choose to give in to self-harm, you are actually giving control of your life to your enemy, the devil (also known as Satan). The enemy wants you to believe that because you are hurting yourself you have some sort of power over your body and over your life. But the Bible says that we are slaves to whatever controls us (2 Peter 2:19).

"Be on the alert. Your adversary, the devil, prowls around like a roaring lion, seeking someone to devour" (1 Peter 5:8, NASB). Satan is your adversary, your enemy. He wants you to believe that you are using self-harm to stay in control of your life, but this is a deception tactic to keep you in bondage. The way to walk in freedom is to choose to surrender control of your life to God instead of trying to control your life yourself.

> *Choosing for the first time to run to God instead of self-harm and saying no to temptation was the hardest thing. But after you choose God over self-harm that first time, every time after that gets easier and easier.*
>
> —Sarah

Both Jessie and Sarah chose to turn to God instead of self-destructive behaviors. When you make the right choice, it brings such freedom! God is always looking for a willing and open heart. You can actually give God control over your life by choosing to surrender to Him the urge to self-injure the moment it begins in you. Just like Jessie, you will soon recognize that you do have a choice about who will be in control of your life.

There are healthier ways than self-harm to handle your intense emotions. Some of these include praise and worship, prayer, reading the Word of God out loud, journaling, and seeking Christian counseling. Later we will discuss in greater detail the power of speaking God's Word out loud so that you can defeat the devil's attempt to keep you in bondage. Prayer is essential no matter how many other things you choose to do to help you walk in freedom. Here's a sample prayer you can use every day to help you stop trying to control your own life and to give control of your life to God:

Prayer of Surrender

Lord, help me to remember that together you and I can handle anything that comes my way today. Instead of giving in to old patterns of coping with overwhelming emotions, I choose to give you control over my life. I ask you to give me wisdom and courage to follow through with my commitment to let you be in charge. I am not willing for my life to stay the same. Today, I take this step: to give you control that I may walk through my day in mental, physical, and emotional peace. Until I have developed this choice to the point where it becomes natural to me, please walk with me through every moment of the day. I will make the choice—you will be my strength. In Jesus' name, Amen!

Forgive Others, Yourself, and God

Is it hard for you to forgive? Are there people you feel anger and bitterness toward as soon as you see their faces? Allowing unforgiveness to take root in your life is a stumbling block to your own freedom.

Forgiving others. The Word of God is clear about forgiveness. Matthew 6:14–15 says, "If you forgive others for the wrongs they do to you, your Father in heaven will forgive you. But if you don't forgive others, your Father will not forgive your sins" (CEV). When you hold tightly to unforgiveness, you open the door to oppression that will hinder your walk to freedom. The Bible also teaches this principle in Matthew 18:23–35. Jesus tells the story about a servant who was released from a large debt of money he owed, however the servant refused to forgive others the money they owed him. When he was found out, he was locked up and tormented. Like the servant, we've been forgiven a great debt—all our sin. Refusing to forgive others after we have been forgiven locks our pain inside of us. Instead, choose to forgive so God can begin to restore you!

Forgiving someone who hurt, abused, or misused you is not saying that what they did to you was okay or it doesn't matter, but it is having an understanding that you have the power to choose your response. Forgiveness is not a feeling or an emotion; it is a choice to be obedient to God. Again, the Bible says if you do not truly forgive those who have offended you, then God will not forgive you (Matthew 6:15). When we choose to forgive those who have hurt us, we are released from the control of further pain and suffering. Unforgiveness keeps you bound to the control of others and their abuse, and that is the last thing you need when you are looking for healing. Through this process of forgiveness, we are also releasing to God those who have hurt us, believing that they will find lasting freedom in Him as well. True forgiveness involves a heart change, and it begins with a deliberate and intentional choice to forgive.

> *As I finally started to open up, God was able to bring so much healing in my life, especially through forgiving those who had hurt me and replacing the ungodly beliefs I had held onto for so long. I never knew that I could have such a close relationship to my Savior and that He would actually speak to me.*
>
> —Sarah

Holding anger, bitterness, and unforgiveness toward others is only hurting you. These emotions eat away at you on the inside. It often has been said that unforgiveness is like you drinking poison but expecting the other person to die.

If there are people you need to forgive, it would be a good idea to write out a list of their names, read them off as you forgive them, and then destroy the paper when you are through. This is just a symbolic gesture to show that you have released those who have hurt you into God's hands for Him to deal with, and that you will make every effort to continue to walk in forgiveness toward those people.

Remember that forgiveness is a choice and a process. There may be times when you don't feel you have forgiven someone, but as you continue to choose forgiveness, your feelings will line up with what you believe.

Forgiving yourself. Being willing to forgive also includes extending forgiveness to yourself. Self-harm often leaves permanent scars that become constant reminders of your sin. Satan will try to keep you in his trap of guilt and shame, but Jesus has already forgiven you and forgotten your sin. Despite knowing this and accepting Jesus' forgiveness, it can be hard to forgive yourself, but this is a vital step in your healing process.

If you had a lot of student loan debt and someone paid it all off for you, would you continue to send in payments? That sounds ridiculous. But when you self-harm, you are trying to pay for sins, real or imagined, that Jesus' death already paid for. Holding self-hatred and anger toward yourself will simply keep you in bondage. Your feelings may not agree right away, but you can daily make the conscious decision to forgive yourself. Soon your feelings will line up with your actions, and you will see yourself the way that God sees you.

Forgiving God. You might feel that you need to forgive God. Although God did not cause the pain you feel or the actions of others that contributed to your pain, you may have harbored disappointment, hatred, and bitterness toward Him. Where was He when you needed Him? Ask God to show you where He was during the hurtful situations of your life, because He was there; He promises that He will never leave you or forsake you (Hebrews 13:5). God may answer by showing you how He intervened and prevented even more harm from occurring. As you come to know the great love God has for you and to understand His character of love and mercy, it becomes possible to let go of the disappointment, hatred, and bitterness you once felt.

Your anger can never punish anyone. Romans 12:19 says, "Don't insist on getting even; that's not for you to do. 'I'll do the judging,' says God. 'I'll take care of it'" (MSG). He will deal with those who have hurt you. Let God turn your scars into a testimony of the freedom that only He can bring.

Here's a sample prayer you can use as you work through forgiving others, yourself, and God.

Prayer of Forgiveness

Lord, I come before you right now and I ask you first to forgive me for holding unforgiveness and bitterness in my heart. I see my need for your healing in my life in this area. Right now I choose to forgive everyone who has hurt me. I forgive them for anything they have done to hurt me. I release them right now, in Jesus' name. I ask, Lord, that you would bless them and that they would come to know you deeply. I choose to forgive right now, even if I don't feel it, because I know your Word says that if I forgive I will be forgiven.

I also forgive myself for making wrong decisions, for turning from you, Lord, and for holding unforgiveness in my heart. And Lord, I know you never caused any bad thing to happen to me in my life, but I blamed you, and I forgive you right now. James 1:17 says, "Every good and perfect gift is from above, coming down from the Father of the heavenly lights, who does not change like shifting shadows." Thank you, Lord, for forgiving me as I have chosen to forgive others. Help me to walk in forgiveness every day. In Jesus' name, Amen.

Believe the Truth

Your thoughts are very powerful. Proverbs 23:7 says that as a person "thinks within himself, so he is" (NASB). What do you think about on a daily basis, truth or lies?

If you are constantly thinking about self-harm, then you will fall into that behavior. This same principle applies to every area of your life. If you believe that your day is going to be hard, then everything will seem difficult for you. The key is to take captive every thought that is not godly (that does not agree with the Word of God). "We take captive every thought to make it obedient to Christ" (2 Corinthians 10:5).

You may be thinking *that sounds complicated*, but it means simply to replace ungodly thoughts (lies) with godly truth. For example, when you think that you are worthless, immediately replace that thought with truth from the Word of God, which says that you are valuable and important to Him: "I praise you because I am fearfully and wonderfully made; your works are wonderful, I know that full well" (Psalm 139:14). "Even the very hairs of your head are all numbered" (Matthew 10:30). "I knew you before I formed you in your mother's womb. Before you were born I set you apart" (Jeremiah 1:5, NLT; see also Ephesians 1:4–6).

> *He created every single part of me—every cell that is in my body was planned, designed, and made by God before I was born. I was a dream of His, and every single part of me was on purpose. Every freckle and every hair on my head was divinely created, and He calls me His masterpiece. He smiled when He finally put His dream and His plan into action and I was created.*
>
> —Rochelle

At this moment, it may be difficult for you to believe God's truth because you have accepted lies about yourself for such a long time. But as you speak the truth over yourself, it becomes life within you and changes you from the inside out. God's Word is like a seed planted deep within your soul. As you faithfully replace these lies with the truth, the seed begins to grow and bloom inside you. You will begin to see your mind-set change. Psalm 103:20–21 tells us that God watches over His Word to perform it.

Do not be discouraged if this process does not happen overnight. It will take some time to renew your mind with God's truth to replace all the lies you have believed. Just be patient with yourself, because God is patient with you. He is full of love, mercy, forgiveness, and abounding grace.

CUT

The Armor of God

Ephesians 6 says to put on the whole armor of God to fight the enemy. Putting on the armor of God is a metaphor the Bible uses to explain vital aspects of our relationship with God and how we are to use them to protect ourselves against attacks from the enemy. The armor of God consists of six pieces—five for protection and one for attack.

The first is the *helmet of salvation*, which represents asking Jesus into your heart and life. Accepting Jesus Christ as your Savior is the first step in winning your battle against self-harm.

The second piece of God's armor is the *breastplate of righteousness*. Second Corinthians 5:21 says that God made Christ "who knew no sin to be sin for us that we might become the righteousness of God in Him" (NKJV). When you ask for forgiveness for your sins, there is an exchange that takes place—God takes your sin and you receive His righteousness.

The *shield of faith* is the part of the armor used to protect you from Satan's attacks. The Bible says in Ephesians 6:16 that this shield of faith literally quenches every fiery dart of the wicked one (his lies, temptations, and the trouble he brings into your life). Practically speaking, when you put your faith in God, no matter what happens, you can trust that if God is for you, who can be against you (Romans 8:31)?

The *belt of truth* means that you have chosen to align your life with the Word of God. This represents everything being held together by the ultimate truth, which is believing in and conforming your life to God's Word.

The next piece of armor is *shoes*, or "symbolically wearing the gospel of peace on your feet" (Ephesians 6:15, NKJV). This means that no matter what happens in life, when you put your trust in

God you can literally walk in the peace of God that passes all understanding (Philippians 4:7). Again, Romans 8:31 says that if God is for you, who can be against you? Even when things appear to be bad, you can trust that God can turn them around for your good.

Last but not least, the *sword of the Spirit* is the Word of God. The Word of God is your weapon. As you speak the Word of God, God watches over His Word to perform it. When the enemy comes to try to bring into your life something that is not God's will, rise up and speak the Word of God. For example, if fear tries to hit you, you can set a firm boundary and say no! Second Timothy 1:7, "God has not given me a spirit of fear, but of power and of love and of a sound mind." When we are afraid or in any other situation, we have the opportunity to take God's Word and boldly proclaim, declare, and decree what the Word says in the face of what may seem or feel totally opposite. The Word of God is the weapon we use to go on the offense against the enemy. The Bible says that when we declare and decree something according to God's will, God will establish it for us! (See Job 22:28; 1 John 5:14.)

It may not be easy to resist acting out your thoughts, emotions, and choices through self-harm, but God's Word planted on the inside of you will actually change your desires and transform you into the person God wants you to be (Romans 12:1–2). As you put the Word on the inside of you, it grows stronger and stronger, and you will be able to fight wrong desires and overcome the enemy. The next time you find yourself struggling with the desire to self-harm, or to do anything that is not of God, remember that God has equipped you with power and strength to finish the fight victoriously (Philippians 2:13). "In all these things we are more than conquerors through him who loved us" (Romans 8:37).

The power of Christ lives inside of you—rise up and speak God's Word! Remember that temptation is designed to lead you into sin. God must be your source, or you will begin to rely on your own strength to cope with life. You may start thinking, *I'm free from self-harm. Why should I worry about falling back into that trap? I would never want to go back.* Just because you have gained freedom does not mean that you are above temptation. Until Satan is convinced that he has no access to you in this area, he will look for ways to trap you again, with self-harm or some other sin. Be careful not to let yourself get tangled up again with what you have fought so hard to overcome. Do not give in to the desires that will invite the devil to make you a slave again.

Galatians 5:1 says Jesus has made you free! Stand in your authority, through Christ, with the Word of God, and do not fall into bondage again. Place the Word of God inside of you and speak it out loud. Remember that though storms may come, God is greater than any temptation!

As a child of God, you have authority over the enemy (Luke 10:19). Exercise that authority by boldly speaking the Word of God to take back the areas of your life where the devil has had you bound (1 John 5:4–5). Don't allow yourself to be defeated. Rise up in Jesus' name and be who you were born to be. Remember, without God, you can do nothing (John 15:5). Allow Him to be your strength.

Replace Ungodly Beliefs

Ungodly beliefs are beliefs contrary to the Word of God about yourself, others, life, and God; they are lies, not the truth. These wrong beliefs rob you of your purpose and take away your hope.

It's impossible to walk in freedom if you are holding on to ungodly beliefs.

You may be asking, "How do I break these ungodly beliefs in my mind?" Confess your sin of holding on to ungodly beliefs and replace them with truths from the Word of God, which we refer to as godly beliefs. For example:

Ungodly belief: I feel empty and incomplete. Hurting myself is who I am and what I do. Without it, I am nothing.

Godly belief: God will open the door to my heart and fill me with love. My identity and my value are found in Him.

Related Scripture: "May you experience the love of Christ, though it is too great to understand fully. Then you will be made complete with all the fullness of life and power that comes from God" (Ephesians 3:19, NLT).

Ungodly belief: I need to self-injure in order to feel release from my pain.

Godly belief: God is my source of healing and strength. I choose to rely on Him to help me through anything I encounter. As I give Him my pain, He will give me the release I need through His peace and healing. I can trust Him to be faithful.

Related Scripture: "You will guard him and keep him in perfect and constant peace whose mind [both its inclination and its character] is stayed on You, because he commits himself to You, leans on You, and hopes confidently in You" (Isaiah 26:3, AMP).

It will help you to begin a written list of your own ungodly beliefs and the godly beliefs and scriptures that you can use to replace them. (Additional examples of godly beliefs can be found at the back of this book.) Read your personal godly beliefs out loud every day for at least a month in the beginning of your walk in freedom. Repetition will help you engrain these godly beliefs into your mind. The practical side of this is that every single day, you'll be making the choice to renew your mind with what God says about you. By doing this, you are literally attacking those lies the enemy has placed within your mind and breaking their power over your life with truth from God's Word.

Remember to be patient with yourself. It took time for those lies to become beliefs in your life. It will take time to get used to taking those thoughts captive and replacing the lies you believe with the truth of God's Word.

The road to freedom is not an easy journey, but you are not alone. Walking in freedom is a process that may be challenging, but it is definitely worth the effort! Be patient with yourself, and do not get frustrated because it takes time. As you renew your mind, God will help you to walk according to what He says about you. Here is a sample prayer:

Prayer of Renewal

Lord, according to your Word in Romans 12:1–2, I will choose to present my body to you God as a living sacrifice, holy and pleasing to you, and I will no longer allow my body to be used as an instrument of sin. I submit to the process of being transformed by the renewing of my mind. I ask you to "search me [thoroughly], O God, and know my heart! Try me and know my thoughts! And see if there is any wicked or hurtful way in me, and lead me in the way everlasting" (Psalm 139:23–24, AMP).

I ask you to help me in this process. Your Word tells me you created me in your image and you desire to set me free in my thinking, feeling, and the choices I make. I want to see myself, others, and you the way I should, and without negativity. I ask for your grace to help me cooperate with you as you renew my mind. The blood of Jesus has redeemed me, and I am forgiven! My body is the temple of the Holy Spirit and I am no longer my own. I belong to you (1 Corinthians 6:19). Thank you for loving me when I have not been able to love myself. As I submit myself to this process, I thank you that I will have victory. In Jesus' name, Amen!

Resist Demonic Oppression

The final step to freedom is dealing with the areas of demonic oppression in your life. Demonic *oppression* is not the same as demonic *possession*. To possess something or someone is to take ownership of it, and Satan cannot own anything that is God's. He does, however, have the right to tempt you. When you become a Christian, asking Jesus to be your Savior, you belong to God. As you submit yourself to God, you can rest, knowing Satan no longer has power over you. You actually have the power to resist the devil and cause him to flee from you (James 4:7).

Whenever we sin, we give Satan an opportunity to have an influence in our lives and create a place where he can rule over us—a *stronghold*. If you are lying about your self-harming behavior, you open the door for the enemy to enter. This applies with any area of willful participation in sin. However, you also have the ability to close the door by choosing to ask for forgiveness and turning away from that sin.

God gave you authority over anything in your life that is not from Him, such as fear, anxiety, and depression. You can live free from the torment of the enemy by no longer tolerating his schemes. If you pray in Jesus' name, Satan is forced to leave. He may try to come back, but stand firm knowing that Satan has nothing in comparison to the authority you have through Jesus. Pray out loud and command the enemy to get out of your life; then get ready for freedom!

These are the steps that will bring you to freedom, but the enemy will constantly attempt to take you in the wrong direction. Remember the truths of God's Word and press on toward the freedom Jesus died to give you. Philippians 3:12–14 says, "I'm not saying that I have this all together, that I have it made. But I am well on my way, reaching out for Christ, who has so wondrously reached out for me. Friends, don't get me wrong: By no means do I count myself an expert in all of this, but I've got my eye on the goal, where God is beckoning us onward—to Jesus. I'm off and running, and I'm not turning back" (MSG). Revelation 20:10 says Satan will be thrown into a lake of burning sulfur, where he "will be tormented day and night for ever and ever." Satan has been defeated; so when he comes back to remind you of your past—remind him of his future! Here is a sample prayer you can use:

Prayer Against Demonic Oppression

Lord, thank you that Satan has already been defeated in my life. I use the authority you have given me and break the strongholds of _____ in Jesus' name. I choose to walk in freedom from this sin and will not give into its temptations. Satan has no power over my life, and I surrender all my thoughts, attitudes, and actions to you alone. I will be ready when the enemy tries to lead me away from your will. I choose to stand firm in the promises you give me in your Word. In Jesus' name, Amen.

Chapter Three

STAYING FREE

As discussed earlier, Satan is a thief, and he has tried to steal something from you—your life! It is okay to be angry about that. God sure is! In fact, He is so disgusted with what Satan is trying to do to His beloved children that He allowed His Son, Jesus, to die an excruciating death to give you authority over the devil. Use that authority you have been given and fight back!

You can say out loud to the devil, "In the name of Jesus, I demand that you get away from me! I will no longer believe your lies, and I choose to believe the truth of the Word of God!" Satan has to listen and obey (James 4:7). The Bible also says, in James 2:19, "You believe that there is one God. Good for you! Even the demons believe this, and they tremble in terror" (NLT). Even the demons know the authority that comes with using the name of Jesus.

Matthew 10:1 says, "Jesus summoned His twelve disciples and gave them authority over unclean spirits, to cast them out, and to heal every kind of disease and every kind of sickness" (NASB). If you have accepted Jesus as your Lord and Savior, then you also are one of His disciples, and you have been given the same power and authority that Jesus gave the original twelve. Use that authority and claim your freedom!

Become Desperate

Are you truly tired of living in the bondage of self-harm? Really consider your answer to that question! Many girls feel that they want to stop hurting themselves but are not willing to do what it takes to be free.

Harmful behaviors feel safe when they are the only behaviors you know to turn to. Battling self-harm tendencies means taking desperate measures at times.

There was a time when the only thing I could think about was cutting, but I wanted freedom more. In my desperation, I sat on my hands and through tears cried, "Help me, Jesus" over and over, until the urges passed and God filled me with His peace.

—Aubrey

When you first begin to choose not to give in to the urges to self-harm, the battle is intense and the emotions are hard to control. As you turn to God, you will find that the peace and comfort He brings you surpasses any of your old behaviors. God does not promise you it will be easy, but He does promise He will bring you through and His reward is beyond anything you can imagine.

Becoming desperate may mean that when you want to hurt yourself, you call a trusted, mature Christian and talk about your struggle. It may mean that you refrain from being in a place where you are alone. It also may mean that you prepare ahead of time and eliminate specific things from your room or from your social environment that would cause you to struggle.

If I am struggling, I cannot be alone; I need to surround myself with support and put myself in the Word of God. I cannot have certain objects just sitting around my room that may not bother other people but are a temptation to me. When I allow myself to stop seeking God first in everything I do, that is when I struggle.

—Sarah

Perfection is not expected! Regardless of your imperfections, continue to move forward toward complete freedom. Let Philippians 3:12–13 encourage you: "Not that I have already attained, or am already perfected; but I press on, that I may lay hold of that for which Christ Jesus has also laid hold of me. Brethren, I do not count myself to have apprehended; but one thing I do, forgetting those things which are behind and reaching forward to those things which are ahead, I press toward the goal for the prize of the upward call of God in Jesus Christ" (NKJV). Notice how the words *reaching* and *press* are used to illustrate the attitude you need to attain freedom.

Picture a baby who is not old enough to walk or crawl, trying to grab something just out of her reach. The baby will strain with all her might. She turns red and may even cry out of desperation. Her father hears the baby's cries and brings the object within her reach. Your heavenly Father will do the same for you! It is important to remember that if a person gives in to temptation and falls, he or she needs to shake off discouragement and continue seeking freedom.

Be Open and Vulnerable

Living in bondage to self-harm is a very dark and lonely place to be. You may be displaying a strong and distant appearance to keep others from being too close and discovering your secret. Isolation may seem like it is the only way to escape the condemning responses you expect from your friends and family. In turn, you may be isolating yourself from God, expecting the same condemnation from Him that you have experienced from others. To be vulnerable to anyone seems terrifying. Being vulnerable is often directly linked to being hurt. But God brings a different aspect to this word and uses your vulnerability as an opportunity to restore all that you have lost!

If your heart and mind remain closed to anything but your own destructive thoughts, emotions, and behaviors, you will always stay trapped in them. When you open yourself up to God and Christian counsel, however, you are allowing light to flood into the darkness of your addiction. God is that light, but the only way He can come into your life is if you let Him.

People are not perfect and may have hurt you in the past. All people will disappoint you at times, however there are those who are mature and will offer accountability and support. When you find people you trust, it is imperative that you remain honest with them throughout your journey to freedom. When you stop being honest about your struggles, you are once again closing yourself off into the darkness from which you are running. Honesty is vital, and your ability to stay in truth, meditate on truth, and be truthful to others will set you free (John 8:32).

Evaluate Your Relationships

Maintaining freedom from self-harm will depend on whom you choose to associate with. The relationships you choose to make a priority in your life will have a profound influence on you, whether good or bad.

The most important relationship you will ever have in your life is your relationship with God. He is the only one who can break the chains of addiction in your life and renew your heart as you choose to renew your mind. Make God your priority. Get to know Him. Having a relationship with God is never boring or dull. To feel alive and at peace at the same time is very exciting!

Set aside time every day to be with God. Do not be legalistic about this and feel that every day at a specific time you have to meet with God or He will be mad at you. God is a loving God, and He longs to be with you. He is not concerned about a specific time, only that you do spend time with Him every day. This is not for God's benefit, but for yours; He wants you to come to Him every day so He can love on you and give you strength to get through each day.

Stay in communication with God. Having a close relationship with anyone requires constant communication; God is not any different. He is easy to communicate with because He is always there. Talk to Him about how you feel, your day, and your struggles. He loves to spend time with you.

Communication goes both ways in a relationship. When you accept Christ as your Savior, you receive the Spirit of God, which allows Him to speak directly to your heart. He has also given you His written Word. The Bible is the Word of God and your foundation for truth. It is much more than a book of rules, but guidelines to live by for your benefit. God does not want to "take" anything from you, such as fun or freedom—He is the source of true joy and eternal freedom. The freedom offered by the world leads to bondage and a life of misery. The Bible offers stories that reveal the true character of God and the path to a life of purpose, peace, and total fulfillment.

The people you associate with have a great influence on you. Being in a close relationship with someone who does not know God or who encourages behavior that is not godly could be a pitfall for your walk in freedom. Some of your relationships may need to be severed permanently; others may just need to be limited. Breaking ties with people does not mean that you are judging or condemning them. You are making a decision to do whatever it takes to break free from the addicting cycle of self-harm, including setting firm boundaries. Pray and seek counsel from a mature Christian to help you know how to handle each individual circumstance or relationship you are unsure of.

Surround yourself with people who love God and seek after Him. Have at least one person in your life to whom you are accountable. You need a safe outlet for sharing what you are going through, so find mature Christian friends and counselors who understand your struggle and can offer godly counsel and advice.

Make a list of names and numbers to call when you are tempted. Talking with someone who is holding you accountable is a great tool at those times. Don't be overly dependent on others, but do not isolate and try to be too self-sufficient. You will need accountability. Do not be silent about what is going on!

Getting involved in a healthy church is also essential to your growth. You need a place where you are under healthy spiritual authority. You need to be where men and women of God can hold you accountable and encourage you in your gifts and callings. It is important for your growth that you sit under solid Biblical teaching to sharpen your character and equip you to stay free.

Hebrews 10:25 says, "Some people have gotten out of the habit of meeting for worship, but we must not do that. We should keep on encouraging each other, especially since you know that the day of the Lord's coming is getting closer" (CEV). This same verse in the *Amplified Bible* uses the phrase "warning, urging, and encouraging one another." Not only will being in a healthy church help you stay free, but it will equip you to go out into the world to help others who are in bondage just as you were. Second Corinthians 1:4 says, "He comforts us when we are in trouble, so that we can share that same comfort with others in trouble" (CEV).

Here are several signs of a healthy church:

- Messages promote and challenge spiritual growth through the Word of God
- Congregation welcomes visitors and newcomers
- Praise and worship allow God to flow freely
- Leadership empowers the church body to become involved and connected with various ministries, such as small groups, missions, and youth or children's ministry
- Provides Bible studies and/or small groups
- Promotes honest and open discussion in small groups to assist in accountability

Prepare for Temptation

You have learned that a heart transformation is needed for freedom; however, the nature of the enemy is to kill and steal. He wants to lure you back into self-harm, and he will try to tempt you so you will fall and be destroyed. Let's look at some ways to prepare for temptation.

James 1:14 says, "Each one is tempted when, by his own evil desire, he is dragged away and enticed." Temptation is something that appeals to the *flesh*, which is a term the Bible sometimes uses to mean the part of our human nature that wants to turn away from God. Rather than allowing your flesh to dictate your actions, follow God's leading. When you make a choice to do what's right, there is a divine strength that rises within you, enabling you to withstand the temptation while choosing to do what is right. The Bible says we need to die to ourselves and our wrong desires (Romans 8:14). This means every time you are tempted and your flesh is drawn toward sin, seek the truth in God's Word and submit that desire to God rather than yielding to the sin.

> *Walking in victory is a continual process of surrendering my life in order to have the life Jesus wants for me. There have been times when I stumbled and fell. Some days are rough, but His grace always abounds when I reach out for it. I have learned that only by going to the cross again and again, and saying no to my flesh is how to live in victory.*
>
> —Jessie

The truth in God's Word can be used to combat feelings of fear and failure. Don't just read the words silently; speak them aloud. Declare that you are not a failure because the Bible says in Philippians 4:13, "I can do all things through Christ who strengthens me" (NKJV). You do not have to be afraid of the future because 2 Timothy 1:7 says, "For God has not given us a spirit of fear, but of power and of love and of a sound mind" (NKJV). You can live a life free from fear and worry!

When you begin to be attacked in any aspect of your life, search God's Word to find the truth to overcome your struggle. Stand up to the devil through your authority in Christ. You will no longer be deceived by his lies when you consistently put the truth inside of you. Continue speaking God's Word and memorizing His promises to you. Very soon it will come out of your mouth because the truth will be in you.

Jesus' Example

Jesus actually set the example for us when Satan came to tempt Him in the wilderness (Matthew 4:1–11). Jesus had been in the wilderness without food for forty days and nights. Near the end of that time, Satan approached Him and said, "If you are the Son of God, tell these stones to become loaves of bread" (v. 3, NLT). Jesus was hungry, and He had the desire and certainly the power to create an impromptu meal, but He knew that was not what His Father wanted. Instead, God wanted Jesus to trust and rely on Him. So even after forty days of fasting, Jesus didn't look to earthly food but to fulfillment from the Word of God. Instead of turning the stones into bread, Jesus answered, "People do not live by bread alone, but by every word that comes from the mouth of God" (v. 4, NLT). Jesus was quoting Deuteronomy 8:3.

Then the devil took Jesus to the highest point of the temple and said, "If you are the Son of God, jump off!" (v. 6, NLT). He provoked Jesus more by quoting Psalm 91:11–12: "He will order his angels to protect you wherever you go. They will hold you up with their hands so you won't even hurt your foot on a stone" (NLT). Satan not only tempted Jesus to defy the laws of gravity and to test God, but he used Scripture to do it! (Satan may use the Word out of context to entice you into choosing your own way rather than trusting God; be prepared!)

Jesus had the Word not only in His mind but also in His heart. He knew He didn't have to test God; He knew God can be trusted. Rather than give in to temptation, He spoke the power of God's Word to overcome the temptation: "The Scriptures also say, 'You must not test the LORD your God'" (v. 7, NLT). Here Jesus was quoting Deuteronomy 6:16. He knew He could depend on God to be faithful to His Word and to follow through on the promises written there.

The devil tried one more time to get Jesus to sin (vv. 8–9, NLT). He took Jesus to the peak of a very high mountain and showed Him all the kingdoms of the world and their glory. "I will give it all to you," Satan said, "if you will kneel down and worship me." Jesus' refusal was clear: "Get out of here, Satan." And He added a third quote from Deuteronomy 6:13: "You must worship the LORD your God and serve only him" (v. 10, NLT). Jesus clearly stated that He would not worship anyone or anything except God. When Satan entices you to worship other gods, such as your body, follow Jesus' example and defeat temptation with the Word of God. Here is a sample prayer you can use:

Prayer for When I'm Tempted

Lord, I come to you open and willing to share my struggles. I ask you to help me resist temptation. Lord God, your Word says that you will not allow me to be tempted beyond what I can endure, and with the temptation you will always provide a way of escape so that I will be able to withstand it (1 Corinthians 10:13). So I ask for your wisdom. I repent of any way I have opened the door to the enemy, and I choose to resist this temptation and receive your help. In Jesus' name, Amen.

Chapter Four

STORIES OF MERCY

*I*t can be easy to *say* that you desire healing. Who does not want to be free from living in pain and suffering? The question is, are you trying to gain freedom in your own strength or in the strength God gives?

In order to receive complete restoration, you must surrender entirely to God. James 4:7 clearly states, "Surrender to God! Resist the devil, and he will run from you" (CEV). Many times we trust God, going through the motions, but continue to rely on ourselves rather than His ability in us. If this is your situation, the freedom you experience will be temporary. True heart change is the only way freedom can be maintained.

A heart change occurs when you realize who you are in Christ and how great and unconditional His love is for you. It's not that you know it just in your mind, but also that you recognize it and believe it in your heart. You experience personally that Christ is real and that He lives in you. If you know this and believe this, then you can walk out your freedom in the strength God gives. When you reach this point, you will remain free from self-harm because you have received the revelation that your body is the temple of the Holy Spirit and God lives in you, and you lose the desire to self-harm. You actually begin to appreciate your body and to care for it.

True heart change—transformation—comes from understanding that the blood of Christ has cleansed you and that God's mercy and grace (His undeserved favor) is a gift. Neither of these is something you earn or deserve. There is nothing you can do to attain freedom outside of receiving it from the Lord. Realize you can do nothing, be nothing, and say nothing that will produce permanent freedom in your life apart from God's mercy and grace. When you experience and begin to live a transformed life, it is because you are grounded in the Word and surrendered in your relationship with God. Nothing will be able to shake that foundation.

In secular treatment, the focus is on changing behavior, which is only temporary. There may be structure, support, and counseling, but there is no real heart change. Behavior modification is not the answer; it is only an outward change, not an inward transformation. As you shift your focus from your struggle to the sacrifice Jesus made for your freedom, true and lasting change will occur. How? As you surrender to Him, He will begin to change your heart and your innermost desires. He is able to help you because He created you. As your desires begin to change, so will your choices and decisions. You will be transformed from within (Romans 12:2). But if you leave God out and try to attain freedom in your own strength, you will be greatly frustrated and will continually be controlled by self-harm.

Satan's plan for you is destruction, but Jesus came that you might have abundant life. In Him all things are possible. He knew you before you were even in your mother's womb. He has a plan for you (Jeremiah 29:11; John 10:10). He sees your potential and has hope for you to reach that potential. He created you and knows that you are able to fulfill your purpose on this earth, but only through Him can you do it. Walk with the God who made you and knows you better than you could ever know yourself. Let Him walk you through this journey.

Julia, Alexis, and Danielle are three girls who were entangled in the lies of self-harm. They were sick of living in darkness and became desperate enough to put everything else aside in order to find freedom and their true identity in Jesus Christ. The road was far from easy for all three girls, but their determination and willingness to allow Him to transform them has led to radically changed lives filled with hope and purpose. God is no respecter of persons (Acts 10:34). What He does for one, He will do for all. May these three stories of mercy bring you hope!

Julia's Story

It started out as an accident, really. I was eight years old and dealing with so much hurt and anger. While doing the dishes, I cut myself on some broken glass. For the first time, I felt a moment of freedom from the pain inside, and at the same time it kind of broke through the numbness. I felt alive, almost normal.

Gradually it escalated from "accidents" to very intentional actions. For me it was important, and a bit obsessive, to see the blood. Seeing the blood made me feel like I was purging all the bad from within me. Self-harm was easier to deal with than what was going on inside. The outside pain hurt a lot less than the inside pain, and the cutting distracted me from what was bottled up. It also made me feel real. I'd numb out and feel like I wasn't living but rather watching some movie play out in front of me. Self-harm somehow confirmed that I was not dead, and cutting became a part of me. It became my identity.

The self-harm was just a symptom to what was going on inside my head and inside my heart. Before I would cut, I would feel numb. Afterward, although I felt relief for a moment, cutting never brought me to where I had hoped. I became a bit scared. How could I hide it? I didn't want to get caught, so I would take a step back from people and withdraw from the world. I hated God. I didn't think He was interested in me. Why would He want to help me now? He didn't help me in the past. I believed God was far off and uninvolved.

Freedom from self-harm started with my belief system. I had to get to know God for who He is. It wasn't about who I thought He was or who others said He was. I had to give God a clean slate to show Himself to me. From there I was able to move forward. It took a lot of strength and courage. I had to face a lot of dark places in myself and deal with things inside of me that were difficult.

I did not do it alone; God was there to walk right beside me, and He brought people to me who understood how to help me. I began to understand who I was in Christ, and continuing to self-harm did not line up with my new identity. I finally understood that I was worth more than that. I couldn't stand there and say how precious I was to God and in the next breath say that I was a cutter and deserved to be hurt.

Self-harm had become like a friend to me. It was what I went to when I was hurting; it was there for me. Not that I am saying that it was in any way helpful, but I almost had to grieve the loss of it. I was no longer a cutter. My identity had to come from something else. Jesus one day asked a cripple if he wanted to be well. You would think it would be an obvious yes, but to be well means to give up the crutches and stand on your own two feet. Standing on my "legs" was hard at first. Strengthening the necessary muscles took time, and some days it was a bit painful. I had to learn to do things differently.

For starters, I had to learn how to let myself cry and feel the pain from past events. Again, God was with me, and after I acknowledged the pain and let myself feel it, God was able to heal it. I also had to learn to express my feelings in ways that weren't hurtful to me or anyone else. For me, expression came through journaling, poetry, singing, and art. I also had a few key Scriptures that I chose to cling to. Even when my feelings told me differently, I was determined to hang on to the truth. One of the passages that served as a lifeline for me was Isaiah 53:3–4: "He was despised and rejected by men, a man of sorrows, and familiar with suffering. Like one from whom men hid their faces. He was despised, and we esteemed him not. Surely He took up our infirmities and carried our sorrows."

Ultimately, you have to go to God for help. He really is there and He really does care. No one else can do it for you, but *you* can do it.

Alexis' Story

My self-harm began when I was thirteen, in a desperate attempt to control and handle the intense emotions I was feeling. I was so angry I just picked up something and began hurting myself without even realizing what I was doing, and I discovered that it made me feel better temporarily. I was in a place of such deep self-hatred, and I used cutting as a way of punishing myself and trying to pay for the wrong things I had done. As it progressed, I got to the point that any time I had an intense emotion such as anger, stress, or sadness, I would hurt myself to try to express the pain I was feeling on the inside. I thought that if I could see it on the outside, the pain would go away or I could at least handle it.

Sometimes I was completely numb and just wanted to feel something. Afterward, I felt the immediate rush of relief and satisfaction that I had punished myself, but immediately following was a wave of guilt and shame because I knew what I was doing was hurting my family and was ultimately wrong. Also, subconsciously, it was a way to get back at them for hurting me.

At this point I was very angry with God. I had grown up in a pastor's family and knew all the Bible stories and all the right things to say, but I had no concept of a relationship with God. I felt like He had abandoned me and was angry with me for the things I was doing. I felt like I had to be perfect in order to earn His love, and I was tired of trying.

I thought that self-harm was a way to secretly control what I was feeling and still be able to present a perfect front to everyone else. I thought it would make life easier and was a way to pay for my sins. I was actually accomplishing nothing except adding more guilt and shame to what I already felt. It also left me with many scars that serve as a constant reminder of what I've done and the darkness I was in.

My family and friends no longer knew how to handle me or what to say to me. Things were always strained and uncomfortable. I was also dealing with an eating disorder at the time, so relationships were very tense. My family was always trying to protect me, and I was constantly looking for ways to get away with things. Most, if not all, of the trust between me and my family was lost. It broke their hearts to see me destroying myself, and it brought so much pain to them. I had very few friends, but the ones I did have felt very uncomfortable and unsure around me.

As I began to discover God's unconditional love for me, it made me realize how much it hurt Him when I resorted to self-harm. I began to realize that there were other ways to release my feelings, and that those feelings were not a bad thing. God also showed me that my body belongs to Him. He made me and He values me. I need to honor my body because God gave it to me. He already paid for my sins on the cross, and nothing I can do to myself can make me more worthy or less a sinner. He loves me because of my imperfections because when I am weak, He can be strong. He forgave and forgot my sin at the cross and does not expect me to continue paying for it.

As God showed me these truths, I had to choose to believe them over my feelings, and only then did I have the strength to resist self-harm. I fell in love with Jesus as I realized His love for me, and now that I have an intimate relationship with Him, it is almost impossible to engage in self-harm because I know how much it hurts Him. He has shown me I am fearfully and wonderfully made, He made me the way I am for a reason, and He loves what He put in me.

Danielle's Story

I began cutting when I was twelve years old. The truth about the sexual abuse I had endured throughout my childhood had been brought to the surface and along with it a flood of confusing emotions. I was angry, hurt, and confused; I felt exposed, betrayed, and not believed. Anytime I tried to express my emotions, they were dismissed as being unacceptable or invalid. The pain became so overwhelming that I did not know how to express it. I began to self-injure using my fingernails or safety pins to cut, or causing deep bruises by hitting myself with hard objects, hoping to find relief. I became frustrated because there was nothing I could do to physically hurt myself enough to compensate for the pain I felt inside.

Soon I began to use sharper objects such as glass and razors to cut in order to draw more blood. The sight of the heavy blood sent a false sense of release to all my emotions. There was something sickly therapeutic about watching the blood drip down and being able to clean it up, doctor it, and make it "better." It was a problem I thought I could fix on my own and stop whenever I wanted. I never told anyone because I believed they would think I was a freak.

Satan distorted the emotions I should have felt for Jesus' blood shed on the cross with the emotions my own self-harm caused. I was consumed with the power I believed shedding my own blood gave me; my eyes were diverted from the cross.

All my self-harm left me with was wounds, yet even as those wounds healed, the needs I thought had been met resurfaced even stronger. I resorted to self-harm again and again for nine years. I felt like I paid a high price, but only accumulated scars and a deep sense of shame. I became very isolated from people and social events. I was terrified of close relationships or any risk of exposing my secret. During an especially difficult time in my life, I realized I could not cut enough to make the pain go away. The only thing to make it disappear was to die. I questioned how much worse hell could be than the life I was living.

After a failed suicide attempt, I was so angry at God because He wouldn't let me die, but I became desperate for a way out. I sought help with a counselor who began to share with me some truths about God and who He really is. I began to read the Bible and was fascinated as I learned how much He loves me despite all of my mistakes. Although I had heard the story of Jesus' death on the cross before, my counselor explained to me that that story was about *me* . . . He died for *me*! I received the revelation of the power of Jesus' blood and found that my blood has no power. He shed His blood to cleanse me from all my sin, shame, pain, and guilt. I learned my emotions and feelings are valid, and that God cares when my heart is breaking. I am never alone in any of my circumstances, good or bad!

God is healing my physical scars and my emotional scars, but right now my physical scars are a reminder of the healing that is taking place. I no longer carry the burden of dealing with my own pain, because I now realize that Jesus bore my pain on the cross so that I wouldn't have to bear it. His heart was broken so that my heart could be healed. His blood was shed for my freedom. He does not want me to shed my blood—He did it for me. I refuse to let the price He paid for me be wasted; I choose to receive *His* sacrifice! If you are struggling with self-harm, would you do the same?

Chapter Five

FOR PARENTS AND OTHERS WHO CARE

There was an urgency in me, and I was waking up with dreams of her in the hospital. I knew she needed help. We had tried everything. We couldn't do it for her. It had to be dealt with and she had to do it. Even though she was young, I knew God would get her through it.

—Jessie's mom

*I*t may seem unimaginable that your daughter or someone else you know and love could struggle with this issue. It is heartbreaking for parents to watch a daughter struggle with self-harm, and feelings of helplessness can consume you as she becomes distant. It is very common for shame and the fight to stay in control to become a wedge between a girl and her parents and friends.

The sooner a problem is recognized, the easier it is to receive help. Self-harming behavior has the potential to spiral out of control quickly, so seek help when signs first surface. Pray and seek God on your daughter's behalf. Seek His guidance, and ask Him to give you the right words to say. Approach your daughter with words of love and truth, and ask God to lead you in His timing. Understand that it is not your role to be Savior or the Holy Spirit in your daughter's life. You are to bring truth and offer support.

Create an Environment for Healthy Expression

Awareness of the problem is the first step to finding the solution. If you ignore what is happening in your family, you will miss the opportunity for a miracle to take place. Once you are aware and willing to look at your surroundings, it is time to start dealing with the problems. It is possible that your daughter has been struggling with hurt for some time.

Creating an environment for healthy expression requires honesty. Your daughter must be allowed to express her feelings openly, without judgment or criticism. If she feels unable to release her negative feelings, she may continue in her destructive habits. You are able to help her by opening a dialogue of love and a genuine attempt to understand her pain. She needs to know that your love for her is limitless before she can accept that your desire for her to get help is sincere.

Generally, girls dealing with self-harm experience immense shame related to their destructive behaviors. They need continual affirmation of acceptance and love. If your daughter perceives that your approval is based on her actions, then you may be communicating the message that your love is conditional. Although you need to confront your daughter's behavior, you must reassure her that you love her for who she is and not her actions.

Reassure your daughter of your belief that she is able to be healed from this pain. Intense shame can lead her to believe "I'm a mistake" and "I'm flawed." The cycle of shame plays a significant role in self-harm, leading your daughter to feel as though it is impossible to turn to God or that she has fallen out of His reach, and because of this she may decide to run away from God. But her problems are not bigger than His love for her. God wants your daughter to turn to Him for refuge and strength. He waits with open arms to help her through this hard time in her life. Romans 8:38–39 says, "For I am convinced that neither death nor life, neither angels nor demons, neither the present nor the future, nor any powers, neither height nor depth, nor anything else in all creation, will be able to separate us from the love of God that is in Christ Jesus our Lord." Encourage your daughter to run to God.

In families where a high value is assigned to public reputation, girls tend to feel extreme pressure to portray an image of perfection. Regardless of how well-intentioned the parents are, girls who are consistently reminded of the significance of the "family name" sense extreme pressure to perform. This can result in girls viewing Christianity as leading a perfect life or feeling the strain of keeping up the facade of "the perfect Christian family."

If you feel your daughter may be struggling under this type of pressure, it is important to communicate your realistic expectations for her. If you find yourself holding her to an unrealistic standard of perfection, you may need to adjust your expectations. Romans 3:23 says, "For all have sinned and fall short of the glory of God." Perfection is not something that God intends for us to obtain until we see Jesus face to face. Everyone is in the growth process. No one is without sin except Jesus Christ. If your daughter feels that she does not have permission to have a bad day, face problems, feel sadness, or express anger, she may turn to self-harm to deal with these "unacceptable" feelings. Help her to understand that these feelings are a normal part of being human. Encourage your daughter to share how she really feels, free from the pressure to perform or to appear perfect. She may believe many lies about herself and have little understanding of her identity in Christ. Assist your daughter in identifying the truth of who she is within the Word the God.

In addition, your daughter may act in ways that mask the root of the true problem. Examples might include general defiance, not fulfilling her responsibilities, exploding in anger over a seemingly ordinary request or withdrawing completely and becoming unusually passive. If your daughter demonstrates this type of behavior, take the necessary time to process through your own feelings instead of reacting out of anger. It is more effective to approach your daughter from a calm perspective than with a heated disposition. Ask her if she is dealing with something else inside instead of automatically criticizing her outward behaviors. Remind your daughter of your love for her even if you do not agree with her behavior.

Confront with Care

It is not uncommon for girls to minimize or even hide their self-harming behaviors from parents and loved ones. Sometimes girls do not even realize the seriousness of their struggle with self-harm. If you recognize your daughter struggling with the signs and symptoms of self-harm, it is important to confront her from a place of love and concern for her well being.

Confrontation can be a beautiful expression of love if approached in the correct manner. Supportively confronting your daughter about her behavior relays the message that you care enough to help her. If you mentally prepare before the confrontation, there is a better chance of positive results.

To prepare for the discussion, ask God to reveal His heart on the matter. If you are married, consult with your spouse about your daughter. It is always best to approach situations from a place of unity with your spouse, and you will be a great source of support for one another throughout the healing process. If you are a single parent, know that you are not alone. God is with you, and He will provide additional support for you.

Once you are prepared to speak with your daughter, ask her to talk with you in a neutral environment conducive to open communication. Ensure privacy and approach your daughter in a nonthreatening way. Begin the meeting with prayer, inviting the Holy Spirit into your discussion. Share honestly about your love and concern for your daughter. Be prepared for the possibility that she may not be receptive to this conversation immediately and may deny her behaviors, and calmly share your reasons or observations. Remind your daughter that you love her so much you are unable to ignore her obvious hurt. Present your daughter with resources to help her find freedom, such as speaking with a pastor, a youth pastor, or a Christian counselor. Reassure your daughter that you want her to find healing and that you are committed to doing whatever it takes to support her in the process.

Be a Support

You must understand that self-harming behaviors are an outward expression of an inward hurt, which can stem from a variety of root issues. However, your daughter's struggle with self-harm does not indicate that you are a bad parent. Many factors can contribute to this behavior, and blaming yourself for your daughter's struggle does nothing to help the situation. Satan uses feelings of guilt and failure to prevent you from providing godly support to your daughter. Be proactive in helping your daughter recognize that God will be your strength as well as hers throughout this difficult process.

In your interactions with your daughter, always remember to take time to seek God first. You will be tempted to lash out at her from your own hurt, anger, or irritation during this journey toward healing, but submit your feelings and concerns to God. He will meet you where you are and carry you through this difficulty.

Nothing is impossible with God. When you are overwhelmed, take a moment and remember the love for your daughter that is motivating this fight. Taking time to consider what is happening with your emotions and gaining proper perspective will help you in your attempts to support your daughter.

We all make mistakes in our interactions with one another. Just as there are no perfect daughters, there are no perfect parents. If you respond to your daughter out of anger, be quick to repent and ask the Lord's forgiveness. In addition, be honest with your daughter about the circumstances and ensure her that your intention was not to hurt her. She will respect your honesty and this will further facilitate open and honest communication between you. The best way to help you daughter be honest and vulnerable is to be an example for her. Humility creates an environment for God's Spirit to move freely without barriers or walls.

Memories of bandaging a childhood injury and making everything okay will come rushing back, and you will long for those days of simplicity. Helplessness is a common feeling among parents with daughters battling self-harm. Know that your love and support are needed, but they are not enough to win your daughter's battle. As a loving parent, it is difficult to remember that you are not her Savior, nor are you capable of having the answer at all times. In order to successfully overcome self-harm, ultimately your daughter must turn to the healing power of God in her life. Only when you understand that it is ultimately God's touch that will heal your daughter will you be able to fully support her journey toward healing.

Seeking support for yourself and for your entire family, through a pastor, counselor, or trusted mentor, can be essential to the overall well-being of your family. As your daughter begins to deal with the root issues behind her desire to self-harm, stressful situations are likely to arise. Ultimately, God is greater than any struggle you or your daughter will encounter. Place Him first in your family and allow Him to show His faithfulness in making a seemingly impossible situation possible. "With God all things are possible" (Matthew 19:26).

A Prayer for Parents

Lord God, I pray for my daughter. I lift her up to you and pray for your Holy Spirit to lead and guide her. I pray for her to know she is loved and accepted by you. I thank you in advance for healing her of her pain. I pray that you would empower her with your Spirit to overcome her desire to self-harm. I pray that she would see her value and importance on this earth. I pray that she would live and not die, declaring the works of the Lord.

Lord God, I surrender my daughter to you. Lead and guide me as I help my daughter. I surrender my life to you. I choose to trust you in all of your ways and trust that you will do a miracle in my family. In Jesus' name, Amen.

GODLY BELIEFS FOR YOUR WALK IN FREEDOM

*U*ngodly belief: No one knows who I really am or how I feel. No one knows how much I hurt inside.

Godly belief: God knows better than anyone exactly what is in my heart. He knows me better than I know myself. I can trust Him to handle me and my heart with the loving hands of healing (Jeremiah 1:5; Psalm 130:2).

Ungodly belief: Life is too difficult and confusing. It will never make sense. No one will stand by me or help me out of the turmoil I am in.

Godly belief: God is bigger than anything life brings my way, and I can choose to trust Him to help me sort it out and see me through. He is faithful (1 Corinthians 1:9; Psalm 61:2).

Ungodly belief: I must experience pain to pay for the horrible things I have done.

Godly belief: Jesus Christ has done everything needed to "take care of" anything in my past, present, and future. When He allowed himself to experience the cross, He paid the penalty for whatever I might do (2 Corinthians 5:21).

Ungodly belief: I have been through too much and suffered too much and been rejected too many times. I cannot trust anyone ever again.

Godly belief: Trust is a gift from God that I choose to accept. He will protect my heart and show me those who are trustworthy (Psalm 5:11).

Ungodly belief: It is my body and what I do to it does not matter. I can hurt it in whatever way I want. God doesn't care.

Godly belief: God fashioned and formed my body, and as His child I belong to Him. My body is the temple of the Holy Spirit (1 Corinthians 6:19).

Ungodly belief: I am so ashamed of the bad things I have done. There is no way I can be forgiven or loved ever again.

Godly belief: God chooses to cover me with the blood of Jesus. I can stand before Him without shame (Romans 8:1; 2 Corinthians 5:21).

Ungodly belief: I will never change. I will always make the same mistakes and continue in the same wrong patterns.

Godly belief: I am a completely new person with Christ. The mistakes of the past are erased, and He gives me the strength to live freely each day (2 Corinthians 5:18).

Ungodly belief: I just cannot stop hurting myself; I just don't have it in me. I cannot live the life God wants me to live; I just don't know how.

Godly belief: If I call on Him, God will provide a way of escape. He is my ever-present help in times of trouble and gives me what I need to do His will and live a godly life (1 Corinthians 10:13; Psalm 121; 2 Peter 1:3).

Ungodly belief: I feel empty and incomplete. Hurting myself is who I am and what I do. Without it I am nothing.

Godly belief: God will open the door to my heart and fill me with love. My identity and my value are found in Him (Ephesians 3:19; Colossians 2:10).

Ungodly belief: I am condemned to hell because I keep making the choice to hurt myself and I cannot stop. God would never allow me to go to heaven. I don't deserve to be saved.

Godly belief: The blood Jesus shed opens the door for me to become a child of God and gain freedom. He died so I could spend eternity with Him in heaven (Colossians 1:13).

Ungodly belief: God could not love someone like me; I am a reject and a loser who only knows how to hurt myself and others.

Godly belief: I am chosen by God to be His child. Nothing can separate me from His love (Colossians 3:12; Romans 8:38–39).

Ungodly belief: Life is too hard, and there is too much pressure to handle. I have to cut; it is the only way I can relieve the pressure and stress.

Godly belief: I can cry out to God anytime. He will be strong in every area of life and lead me to safety. There is nothing that will come my way today that God and I cannot handle together (1 Peter 5:7; Matthew 11:28; Psalm 61:2).

Ungodly belief: I will never be able to stop hurting myself. It is too hard, and I am too weak.

Godly belief: With God inside me, empowering me, I can change (Philippians 4:13).

Ungodly belief: I am a bad person. If I do not change, God will wash His hands of me, and I will be on my own to deal with life.

Godly belief: Jesus Christ will never give up on me; His mercies are new every morning (Hebrews 13:5; Lamentations 3:22–23).

Ungodly belief: I have hurt myself for too long and have too many ugly scars. I will never stop doing this. I see no way to solve the problem.

Godly belief: I am more than a conqueror through Jesus Christ. With His help I can overcome any obstacle (Romans 8:37).

Ungodly belief: I have to be a certain way or the way others think I should be in order for them to love and accept me.

Godly belief: God created me special and unique, and He loves and accepts me exactly as I am (Psalm 139:13–14; 1 Peter 2:9–10).

Ungodly belief: If I do not do things like hurt myself, I will not be noticed. I am always overlooked by others.

Godly belief: God sees me, and I am more important to Him than anything else in this world (Matthew 10:29–31).

Ungodly belief: I have to be in control to make sure that all my needs are met.

Godly belief: I trust that God loves me enough to provide for me and give me a fulfilled life. God promises not only to meet my needs but to give me the desires of my heart (Philippians 4:19; Psalm 37:4).

Ungodly belief: I should never have been born, because I serve no purpose in life. I was a mistake.

Godly belief: God planned every moment of my life even before I was ever born. He has created an amazing destiny for me (Jeremiah 1:5; Psalm 139).

Ungodly belief: Everyone gives up on me because I cannot seem to change. I am a loser and deserve whatever happens to me.

Godly belief: God is never disappointed in me, and with Him change is possible. God is conforming me into His likeness (Philippians 1:6; Romans 8:29).

Ungodly belief: I have to guard my heart and my emotions so I will not get hurt again. I cannot risk being disappointed by others.

Godly belief: God is my shield and the safe place to whom I can run. He will be my protector (Psalm 91).

Ungodly belief: No one loves me, wants me, or cares about me. Hurting myself takes my mind off of the hurt in my heart.

Godly belief: God's love for me is never ending. He heals broken hearts and gives me love that I can share with others (Isaiah 61:1; Luke 4:18; Isaiah 53:4–5).

INDEX TO PRAYERS

REFERENCES

Nancy Alcorn, *Keys to Walking in Freedom* CD series Mercy
  Ministries
  www.mercyministries.com
Neil T. Anderson, *The Bondage Breaker*
  www.ficm.org
Neil T. Anderson, *The Steps to Freedom in Christ*
  www.ficm.org
Charles Capps, *God's Creative Power*
  www.charlescapps.com
Chester and Betsy Kylstra, *Restoring the Foundations*
  www.phw.org

ABOUT MERCY MINISTRIES

*M*ercy Ministries exists to allow young women to experience God's unconditional love, forgiveness, and life-transforming power. We provide residential programs free of charge to young women ages 13–28 who are dealing with life-controlling issues such as eating disorders, self-harm, addictions, sexual abuse, unplanned pregnancy, and depression. Our approach addresses the underlying roots of these issues by addressing the whole person—spiritual, physical, and emotional—and produces more than just changed behavior; the Mercy Ministries program changes hearts and stops destructive cycles.

Founded in 1983 by Nancy Alcorn, Mercy Ministries currently operates in four U.S. states and in Australia, Canada, New Zealand, Peru, and the UK, with plans for additional U.S. and international locations underway. We are blessed to have connecting relationships with many different Christian congregations but are not affiliated with any church, organization, or denomination.

Residents enter Mercy Ministries on a voluntary basis and stay an average of six months. Our program includes life-skills training and educational opportunities that help ensure the success of our graduates. Our goal is to have each young woman not only complete the program but also discover the purpose for her life and bring value to her community as a productive citizen.

For more information, visit our Web site at
www.mercyministries.com.

Mercy Ministries of America

www.mercyministries.com

Mercy Ministries Australia

www.mercyministries.com.au

Mercy Ministries Canada

www.mercycanada.com

Mercy Ministries UK

www.mercyministries.co.uk

Mercy Ministries New Zealand

www.mercyministries.org.nz

ABOUT THE AUTHOR

*A*fter eight years in corrections and social work, Nancy Alcorn began to realize the inadequacy of secular programs to offer real transformation in the lives of troubled girls.

Believing that only Jesus could bring restoration into the lives of girls who were desperately hurting, she knew God was calling her to step out to do something about it.

In 1983 Nancy opened the first Mercy Ministries home, in Monroe, Louisiana. God had instructed her to do three specific things to ensure His blessings on the ministry: to accept girls into the program free of charge, to give at least 10 percent of all Mercy Ministries' donations to other Christian organizations and ministries, and to take no state or federal funding that might limit freedom to teach Christian principles. As Nancy has continued to be faithful to these three principles, God has been faithful to provide for every need of the ministry just as He promised.

Nancy frequently speaks at conferences around the world. She lives in Nashville, Tennessee, which is also the home of the national headquarters of Mercy Ministries.

To order additional copies of this title call:
1-877-421-READ (7323)
or please visit our web site at
www.winepressbooks.com

If you enjoyed this quality custom published book,

drop by our web site for more books and information.

www.winepressgroup.com

"Your partner in custom publishing."